Clara
BARTON
Founder of the American Red Cross

DOROTHY FRANCIS

A Gateway Biography
The Millbrook Press
Brookfield, Connecticut

For Richard

Cover photography courtesy of The Granger Collection, New York
Photographs courtesy of The Granger Collection, New York: pp. 4, 24, 27; North Wind
Picture Archives: pp. 7, 11, 13, 20, 33; Clara Barton National Historic Site: pp. 8, 31, 40;
American National Red Cross: pp. 15, 36; Library of Congress: p. 18; Hulton Getty/Archive
Photos: pp. 23, 29; Brown Brothers: p. 39; © AFP/Corbis: p. 42

Library of Congress Cataloging-in-Publication Data
Francis, Dorothy Brenner.
Clara Barton : founder of the American Red Cross / Dorothy Francis.
p. cm. — (A Gateway biography)
Includes bibliographical references (p.) and index.
Summary: Chronicles the life of Clara Barton, from her early days as a teacher to her work
with the Bureau of Records and her establishment of the American Red Cross.
ISBN 0-7613-2621-9 (lib. bdg.)
1. Barton, Clara, 1821–1912—Juvenile literature. 2. Red Cross—United States
–Biography—Juvenile literature. 3. Nurses—United States—Biography—Juvenile literature.
[1. Barton, Clara, 1821–1912. 2. Nurses. 3. Women—Biography.] I. Title. II. Series.
HV569.B3 F73 2002 361.7'634'092—dc21 [B] 2001044878

Published by The Millbrook Press, Inc.
2 Old New Milford Road
Brookfield, Connecticut 06804
www.millbrookpress.com

Clara Barton stood at one end of her living room in Washington, D.C. She looked at the twenty-one people in her audience. Those people had shown great interest in her idea of starting an American Red Cross Society that would provide people with disaster relief in times of both peace and war.

On that special day, May 21, 1881, Clara did not remind her audience of the years she had spent promoting the Red Cross idea. Instead, she told of the horrors she had seen on battlefields. She told of the terrors of war. She told of fathers, brothers, and sons who had died due to disease and lack of supplies. She begged her listeners to help.

In 1866, Clara Barton posed for this
photograph, which was taken by Mathew Brady.
Brady had become famous for his stirring
pictures of Civil War soldiers and battlefields.

"I want every one of you to get up in turn and say what I should do," she said. "I will drop the Red Cross idea if you refuse to support me."

The first person said, "Go on with your work," and every other person at the meeting agreed.

"Then and there," wrote a guest who was present, "we took an oath of allegiance to the Red Cross. We pledged ourselves to see that the work was carried through."

Three months later, at a meeting in Dansville, New York, Clara organized the first American Red Cross chapter, and twenty-two people became founding members of that new organization.

Clara Barton was born in North Oxford, Massachusetts, on Christmas Day 1821. She had four older siblings, and parents whose frequent arguments caused great tension in the family. Clara's father was so indifferent to her coming birth that he delayed in calling medical help for his wife. Clara arrived before the doctor did. Luckily, Clara was a healthy baby, and the family took this new member in stride. They named her Clarissa Harlowe Barton, but they quickly shortened Clarissa to Clara.

Clara's father, Stephen, was a successful farmer and a former soldier. His war tales may have inspired Clara to help soldiers later in her life. Clara's mother, Sarah, was a fiery-tempered homemaker. Clara could seldom please her, and often found herself a victim of her mother's anger.

Of her four older siblings, Dorothy, Stephen, David, and Sally, Sally was closest to Clara in age. But eleven years separated them. Sally spent much time away at boarding school, and she had little influence on Clara's early life.

When Clara was six years old, her oldest sister, Dorothy, suffered a mental breakdown, and the family kept her at home. Dorothy never regained her health, and her illness haunted Clara all her life, sometimes causing Clara to doubt her own sanity.

Her brother Stephen taught Clara arithmetic, which helped her both in school and in later life. David taught Clara to ride a horse and to play outdoor games. David was her favorite sibling.

Short, plump, and homely were words that some people used to describe Clara as a child. People called her an ugly duckling, and her mother frequently reminded her of her shortcomings. Clara thought her parents favored her brothers and sisters because they

The rural Massachusetts area where Clara Barton was born may have looked something like this. This nineteenth-century scene is of Mount Holyoke, which is about 50 miles (80 kilometers) from Barton's birthplace in North Oxford.

*This photograph of the house
where Clara Barton was born
was taken in more recent years.*

were older and stronger. Sometimes shyness and fear kept Clara from asking for things that she needed, such as new gloves, shoes, or dresses. Many times she felt bitter about the way she was treated.

But early in life Clara learned that she was smart. By age three she could read, and her parents sent her to school. Clara liked school, but it saddened her to realize that her mother enjoyed being rid of her for much of each day.

Schoolteachers liked Clara, but she didn't fit in with her classmates. They teased her about her homely looks and her tomboy ways. School might have been totally unpleasant if it were not for one important thing.

Clara learned that she could win the attention she longed for by using her brain. Teachers praised her reading. They praised her ability to work arithmetic problems quickly and correctly. Clara succeeded in the classroom through hard work and clear thinking. Later, her school memories featured favorite teachers and studies rather than classmates and fun.

Clara constantly searched for her place in the world, afraid she would never find it. Shyness made her avoid people, and once later in life she said, "Of the earlier years of my life, I remember nothing but fear."

In spite of her shyness and her fears, Clara welcomed hard work. She once helped a hired painter paint the family's house. Caring for the farm animals became part of her daily routine. When her brother David suffered severe injuries in a fall from a barn roof, Clara gave up school and nursed him back to health.

While caring for David, she learned to handle the slimy leeches that doctors used in treating patients in those days. She learned to dress blisters and ugly sores. For two years, she cared for David, seldom leaving his side. But when David grew strong again and did not need her constant care, Clara felt useless.

*A*s she entered her teen years, Clara worked in the mill her brother Stephen owned until fire destroyed it. She then looked outside her family for work. She tutored poor children. She nursed the sick during a smallpox epidemic. She liked work where she could help others.

When Clara reached her late teens, her parents consulted a phrenologist to tell her future. By studying the shape of a person's head, a phrenologist made predictions about that person's abilities. Clara's phrenologist said that Clara might be a good schoolteacher.

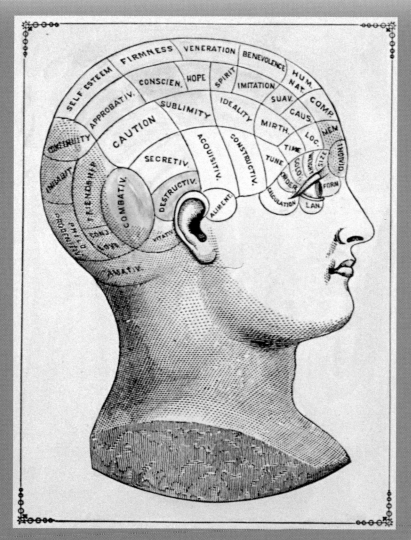

The old-fashioned practice of phrenology taught that different sections of the brain controlled different parts of the personality. Phrenologists felt they could discover many things about a person by studying the bumps on his or her head.

Public Education in the Nineteenth Century

In the 1800s, many children received their education in a one-room schoolhouse. At that time most towns were small, and few children went to school. In a one-room schoolhouse, one teacher taught children from kindergarten through eighth grade. The parents of the town paid the teacher, and sometimes the teacher lived in a pupil's home.

Teachers taught their students reading, writing, geography, arithmetic, grammar, spelling, and oral reading. If pupils were lucky, their teacher could also teach music and art. If not, sometimes artistically talented teachers visited schools once a week to teach those subjects.

The schoolhouses were usually simple buildings with windows in their long walls. Sometimes they had one or two windows by the door. A wood-burning stove provided warmth during the winter. Teachers expected older boys to bring in enough wood each day to keep the woodbin filled and the stove burning.

When towns needed larger schools, many people hated to see the one-room schools abandoned. Many parents liked the strict discipline in those schools. They liked the team spirit among the classmates. They also liked the close relationship their children enjoyed with their teacher. Those schools contributed greatly to a community's social makeup. They offered places where the townspeople could hold elections, picnics, and celebrations.

A student gives a speech in this scene from a nineteenth-century one-room schoolhouse as his teacher looks on, and a fellow classmate stands on a box as punishment for some bad behavior we can only guess about.

Clara said no. She hated the idea of facing strangers in a classroom. However, her family arranged for her to teach. To Clara's surprise, she enjoyed the job. From the start, she let pupils only slightly younger than she was know what she expected of them. She had no discipline problems and was soon in demand as a teacher.

Unlike most girls, Clara saw teaching as a career—not as something to do only until marriage. She put her heart into her work. Her pupils remembered and respected her long after they left her schoolroom. Clara also remembered her pupils. As an old woman she wrote to a friend, "Their lifelong loyal allegiance to me is beyond my comprehension."

After more than a decade of teaching, Clara was about twenty-eight. She wanted to do something different, but she didn't know what. At that time her brother Stephen invited her to be a bridesmaid in his wedding in Maine. That was Clara's first experience traveling far from home. She felt self-conscious about her homeliness, and again shyness and fear controlled her thinking. However, traveling to the wedding proved to be a turning point in her life. In spite of her looks, fears, and shyness, she realized that she could cope with new situations.

Clara Barton at the time she was a schoolteacher

Once back home, Clara still was not sure what she wanted to do next, so she decided to return to school as a student. She enrolled at Clinton Liberal Institute in Clinton, New York. Once again, she didn't fit in with many of her classmates. Some of them considered her strange. She was ten years older than they were. She ate only two meals a day. She wore the same two dresses day after day, week after week.

Clara enjoyed the company of men, and although some men admired her, she wanted only casual friendships, never marriage. Perhaps her parents' unhappy home life influenced her thinking.

At Clinton, she worked hard and earned good grades. But her money ran out, and she never finished her courses. All her life Clara regretted this and felt she had had an incomplete education.

*A*fter dropping out of Clinton Liberal Institute, Clara visited friends in New Jersey. Her thoughts remained on education—free education for all children. Because she felt that every child should have an education, she spoke to school officials in Bordentown, New Jersey, about starting free schools. Clara offered to teach without pay, asking only for a building in which to teach.

A Woman's Place

In the nineteenth century, few jobs were available to women. Money was scarce. Jobs went to men. People felt that a working woman deprived a family man of a job and a livelihood.

It was acceptable for a young woman to be a schoolteacher until she married, but society expected her to marry and raise a family. If she didn't do this, people called her an "old maid." That label suggested that the unmarried woman was either homely or had a bad personality—or both. Most girls tried to avoid the "old maid" label.

Unmarried women faced limited opportunities. Some became schoolteachers. Some became nurses. Others served as nannies in homes where families needed a mother's helper. Often, unmarried women remained at home caring for elderly parents until they became elderly themselves.

Sometimes women who showed talent in arithmetic and writing could find jobs in business offices. Such women were usually daughters or relatives of men already working in these offices. If a woman lacked family connections, she might depend on friends to speak on her behalf and find a job opening for her.

Few people envied the life of a single woman in the nineteenth century.

Finally, the city officials agreed to try Clara's idea. They offered her a contract—with pay. To their surprise, the school became a success. Clara opened the school in the fall of 1852 with many students. When school was over in the spring of 1853, she returned home to Massachusetts feeling independent and successful. But that ended when she returned to her school the next

This photograph of Clara Barton's school in Bordentown, New Jersey, was taken in the 1930s.

fall. School officials had decided that a woman couldn't handle such a successful school.

There was now a man in charge of "her" school. Clara learned that she was to be his female assistant. The man's salary was to be $600; Clara's only $250. Angry and heartbroken, Clara resigned.

She became depressed. Being expected to serve under a man in a school she had fought for, created, and made a success upset her. She lost her voice and became ill. Her family invited her to come home, but she refused to return as a failure at age thirty-two. Resting at the home of friends brought back her spirits and her health, but she no longer wanted to teach school.

*A*fter giving up teaching, Clara moved to Washington, D.C. She had heard that jobs that suited her talents might be available there. A congressman from Clara's home district befriended her, helping her find employment in the U. S. Patent Office. There, Clara received the same salary as men received for doing similar work. She did well in her job because she could write legibly and quickly. Some of the male office workers resented her. They called her the "pest in petticoats," but Clara refused to let them drive her away.

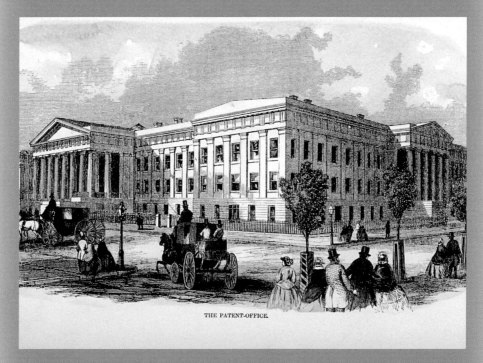

THE PATENT-OFFICE.

A view of the U.S. Patent Office in Washington, D.C., in the 1850s, around the time Clara Barton began to work there

Later Clara wrote of this job: "My arm is tired, and my poor thumb is callused from holding a pen. But my situation is delightfully pleasant."

*I*n January 1861, President Abraham Lincoln took office in Washington, D.C. At that time the question of slavery and human rights threatened peace throughout the nation. On April 12, Confederate soldiers fired on Union soldiers at Fort Sumter. This battle in the harbor of Charleston, South Carolina, marked the start of the Civil War. President Lincoln immediately called for 75,000 volunteers to protect Washington from the Confederate rebels.

The capital city was unprepared for the arrival of so many people. Some of the volunteers arrived needing food, clothing, and shelter. Clara, who always looked for ways to serve others, saw the desperate need of these men. She volunteered to help collect supplies for the soldiers. For two years she worked at this task in addition to doing her job at the Patent Office.

Some people in the Patent Office expressed sympathy for the South. Fiercely loyal to the Union, Clara spoke out against those people. Her views made her unpopular with her fellow workers. When her father died in 1862, Clara went home. While mourning, she had time to consider her choices for future work.

Clara decided that she could be of greatest service to her country by joining the military forces at the battle-fields and tending the wounded soldiers. She had saved her money, and she could support herself for a while without a paying job.

The idea of visiting battlefields attracted few women, but Clara wanted to go to the front. She sought permis-sion from the proper officials, reminding them of her success in helping the troops in Washington. She also pointed out that due to her time spent collecting sup-plies for soldiers, she had access to three warehouses of food, clothing, and hospital supplies—things every sol-dier needed.

Army officials granted Clara permission to nurse the wounded in the Army of the Potomac camped near Fredericksburg, Virginia. Although she had no formal training as a nurse, Clara knew she could use the nursing experience she had gained as a girl when she had nursed her brother David.

Clara boarded a crowded train leaving Washington, traveling with boxes and barrels of supplies. For a bat-tlefield uniform, she wore a plain dark skirt and blouse. When she reached the battlefield, she panicked for a

This photograph is of a Union regiment drilling as they are camped outside Washington, D.C., at the start of the Civil War.

While this dramatic picture of Clara Barton nursing a soldier on the battlefield may have been an artist's creation, she did work tirelessly to tend to the wounded and dying as they were brought in from battle.

moment at the cries of the wounded men. Then she replaced panic with courage as doctors gratefully welcomed the much-needed supplies she brought from Washington.

There was no hospital on the battlefield, only a small train station, Fairfax Station. In that area, wounded and dying soldiers waited for relief and transportation to Washington. Clara prepared food for the men, using jelly jars and wine bottles as dishes. At times she gave her own sandwiches to starving soldiers.

At one time during the four-day battle, she worked for two days and nights without sleep or food. She felt a special sadness when she recognized some of the wounded soldiers as her former school pupils.

Clara always carried a small notebook in her skirt pocket. In it she wrote the names of the dying men. She recorded their last messages for their families. And she shuddered at the sight of such suffering.

"I cannot describe it," she jotted in her diary.

Only moments after the wounded soldiers finally left on the train bound for Washington, rebels set fire to Fairfax Station. Clara's work had saved lives. She had proved her worth to the army, and officials allowed her to follow the troops to Port Lookout, Maryland.

At times, shells burst among the hospital workers, lighting up the sky. Later, Clara wrote, "When I looked into a mirror, my face was the color of gunpowder, a deep blue."

In spite of the chaos, Clara helped surgeons stitch wounds. She helped them perform bloody amputations. She was no longer timid and fearful. As she helped those around her, she gained national acclaim as "the angel of the battlefield."

Clara caught typhoid fever, but after a month's rest, she continued working on the battlefields. Only when her supplies ran out did she return to Washington. By the fall of 1863, her funds were low. Friends sent her money and clothing. The admiration of her friends and of the soldiers she had helped boosted her spirits.

Clara eventually returned to the battlefields, but now army doctors objected. They felt that her bold demands for supplies were a criticism of their methods. They tried to force her from their territory. Their actions angered and saddened her. At that time she was trying to establish a warehouse for her supplies, and that idea failed. For a time, she felt useless.

But in 1864, the army needed her again. At Fredericksburg, Virginia, Union officers had four hundred wounded men and no supplies. Clara came to their rescue and again collected supplies from the public.

Taken in May 1864, this photograph shows wounded soldiers near Fredericksburg, Virginia, around the time Clara Barton was called back by the army to collect supplies for their medical care.

*I*n 1865, Clara learned of soldiers arriving from Southern prisons in terrible condition and needing help in finding their families. Again, Clara saw a need to fill. She went to President Lincoln and won his permission to help released prisoners of war.

President Lincoln wrote a letter that was distributed through the nation's newspapers.

> *To the Friends of Missing Persons:*
> *Miss Clara Barton has kindly offered to search for the missing prisoners of war. Please address her at Annapolis, giving her the name, regiment, and company of any missing prisoner.*
>
> *[signed]*
> *A. Lincoln*

Clara went to War Department headquarters in Annapolis, Maryland. Once there, she could find no official listing of prisoners. War Department officials wondered what to do with this bold woman. At last they lent her a tent and gave her permission to begin her search.

Thousands of letters arrived in response to President Lincoln's letter, each asking for word of a beloved soldier. As Clara opened the mail, she placed each missing soldier's name on a list. Newspapers published the list. She circulated the list through civic and religious organ-

In this painting, a Union soldier dreams of
his homecoming. Clara Barton's work in matching
missing soldiers to their families at the end
of the Civil War helped many soldiers'
and families' dreams to come true.

izations. She also asked veterans to check the list for names they could help her with.

Her plan worked. She received many replies from the families of missing soldiers. Officials then granted Clara the clerks, desks, ledgers, and messengers she needed to establish a Bureau of Records and continue her work of reuniting families.

*I*n the summer of 1865, Secretary of War Edward Stanton ordered that the graves at the war prison at Andersonville, Georgia, be properly marked. Captain James Moore, in charge of battlefield cemeteries, invited Clara and a former prison worker, Dorence Atwater, to go to Andersonville and mark the graves. After much hard work, they completed this difficult task. Government officials chose Clara to raise the flag when they dedicated the Andersonville Cemetery on August 17, 1865.

Clara returned to her Washington office with no funds. Her friend Frances Gage, an activist for women's rights, encouraged Clara to ask Congress for money to continue her work of finding missing soldiers. Clara took that bold step. The first woman to appear before Congress, she asked the lawmakers for money. And they granted her request.

Clara Barton raises the American flag at the dedication of Andersonville Cemetery on August 17, 1865.

Andersonville Prison

In 1863, the Confederate Army planned to build a prison to hold captured Union soldiers. They selected the small village of Andersonville, Georgia, because of its Deep South location and because it lay near fresh water and a railroad. Perhaps they also chose Andersonville because there were so few townspeople to protest the building of a prison.

The prison would cover more than 16 acres (6.5 hectares) and hold 10,000 prisoners. Officials named the prison Camp Sumter, and slaves cleared the land. Slaves also dug ditches for the construction. A stockade fence enclosed the prison and measured more than 1,000 feet (305 meters) long and almost 800 feet (244 meters) wide. Closely fitted pine logs formed its walls, allowing prisoners no outside view.

Workers built another fence 20 feet (6 meters) inside the stockade wall. Officers called the land between the stockade and the inner fence "no-man's-land." They immediately shot any prisoner caught stepping into that restricted area.

Twenty thousand prisoners arrived at Andersonville in the first four months of its operation. Prisoners worked for two weeks to enlarge it. In another two months, the prison population rose to 33,000.

By September 1864, General Sherman's Union troops occupied Atlanta, Georgia. Fearing a Union raid on Andersonville, Confederate officers ordered most of the prisoners transferred to other camps. Only 5,000 prisoners remained at Andersonville when the war ended in April 1865.

During the fifteen-month existence of Andersonville Prison, 13,000 prisoners died of exposure, disease, and malnutrition. After the war, the United States government took over the cemetery near the prison where the dead lay buried and designated it a National Cemetery.

The conditions at Andersonville Prison were harsh. Thousands of soldiers did not make it out alive.

Following the war, the prison grounds fell into private hands. Farmers planted the area with cotton and tobacco. Later, the Grand Army of the Republic of Georgia acquired the land. Officials ordered stone monuments built to mark the prison's corners and gates.

Today, travelers still visit Andersonville to see the site of the notorious prison and go to the cemetery to honor the soldiers who died there.

Clara worked with renewed interest, and to increase her funds, she also began speaking for a fee to groups about her experiences on the battlefield and in her work after the war. Her lectures gave publicity to her and her work of reuniting war-torn families. Historians suggest that Clara sang her own praises because she received so little praise from her family. The Bartons thought it improper for a woman to engage in activities that got her name in the newspaper.

Audiences liked Clara's lectures, but Clara disliked public speaking because she suffered from stage fright. However, she enjoyed receiving $75 to $100 per lecture—the same amount men received. She continued the lecture circuit until 1870, when ill health forced her to stop. She followed her doctor's advice and went to Europe to rest. Her sister Sally traveled with her for two weeks, and then Clara was on her own.

Through her work in Washington, Clara had met diplomats and other influential people. In Geneva, Switzerland, friends invited her to be their guest for as long as she cared to stay. There she met Dr. Louis Appia, who told her about the International Convention of Geneva. People commonly called this convention the

Clara Barton and the Feminist Movement

When the American colonies broke free from England in 1776, men made the laws for the new nation. It came as no surprise that those laws favored men. Even if an unmarried woman owned property and paid taxes, laws prohibited her from voting in an election.

Of course the women protested. They repeated what men had said all along: "Taxation without representation is tyranny." Nobody listened. A century after the American Revolution, men still managed most women's lives.

Women still had no voting rights. Married women could own no property other than the clothes they wore. Married women could sign no legal documents without their husband's permission. No law existed allowing women to divorce abusive husbands. Married women had no control over the money they might inherit or any money they might earn.

In many respects single women were better off than married women. But few jobs were open to single women. Only Clara's determination and the help of her many friends enabled her to find a self-supporting job in Washington, D.C.

Women continued to argue against America's unfair laws. In 1848, Susan B. Anthony and Elizabeth Cady Stanton organized the first women's rights convention. It wasn't until 1867 that Clara Barton met those feminist leaders. Clara supported their desire to expand women's political and social rights. Yet she never allied herself with them too closely.

Clara felt that the suffragists, those working to get women the right to vote, were well organized and that their demands would be granted without her help. She also felt that if she worked too closely with the suffragists, she would be taking valuable time away from her other causes. Clara wanted to do nothing that might hurt her work with released prisoners of war and later, her work in establishing the American Red Cross.

Red Cross. At the time, Clara didn't recognize the importance of this meeting with Dr. Appia.

She said, "I was sure the American people did not know anything about it [the Red Cross] or ever heard of it."

When the Franco-Prussian War broke out in Europe in 1870, Dr. Appia and King William of Prussia asked Clara to help solicit supplies for the soldiers. Clara did this willingly. She also asked to assist at the battlefields as she had done in America. Although officials denied that request, Clara saw the Red Cross in action. The organization's good work deeply impressed her.

Many European officials wanted to thank Clara for her help. Clara returned home in 1873 with a Gold Cross of Remembrance from Germany's Grand Duke of Baden, an amethyst from the Grand Duchess Louise, also of Germany, the Jewel of the Red Cross from Queen Natalie of Serbia, and the Iron Cross of Merit from the emperor and empress of Germany.

Clara Barton received this Iron Cross of Merit from the emperor and empress of Germany for her help during the Franco-Prussian War.

The Red Cross

The Red Cross is an international agency. In times of war, its job is to relieve the suffering of wounded soldiers, civilians, and prisoners of war. In times of peace, the Red Cross gives help to people caught in disasters such as floods, hurricanes, tornadoes, earthquakes, disease epidemics, and famines.

In the nineteenth century, a Swiss philanthropist, Jean-Henri Dunant, initiated the founding of the Red Cross. The almost complete lack of care for wounded soldiers appalled him. He appealed to national leaders to establish societies to aid people wounded in wartime.

In response to his plea, five Swiss citizens formed the International Committee of the Red Cross. This committee issued a call for an international conference to address the problem of caring for those wounded in battle. That first conference was held in October 1863, and it led to the establishment of the International Red Cross.

This Swiss organization inspired Clara Barton's work in establishing the American Red Cross.

She also returned home determined to start a Red Cross organization in America.

Clara fought hard to establish the American Red Cross. She succeeded in 1881, and the group's founding members elected her their president. Other humanitarians soon saw the value of the Red Cross, and Clara had to struggle to keep her place as its leader. Other organizers wanted to form spin-off groups that she felt would weaken the main organization.

"My work was accomplished against fearful odds," she later wrote.

For more than two decades the Red Cross thrived under Clara's strong and efficient leadership. Clara refused to let advancing age limit her activities. She denied dyeing her hair and telling people that she was younger than she really was. But she did those things to make herself seem younger and thus prevent people from saying she was too old for her job.

When she was in her late seventies, Clara sailed to Cuba with a cargo of supplies for the men fighting in the Spanish-American War. At that time, public sentiment began to turn against the Red Cross. People thought it inappropriate for a woman of Clara's age to work in a war zone.

In addition to public criticism of the Red Cross, arguments occurred within the organization. Clara demanded to have her way about all decisions, but top-ranking members insisted that their ideas be considered. Critics accused Clara of being careless with the organization's money. Clara admitted that she wasn't a very good bookkeeper, but she denied that she meant to steal money. She admitted that she sometimes had stuffed bills, checks, and receipts in a box for later consideration, much as she had done while working on wartime battlefields.

This picture shows Clara Barton seated among nurses and others during her trip to Cuba in the late 1890s to assist the Red Cross during the Spanish-American War.

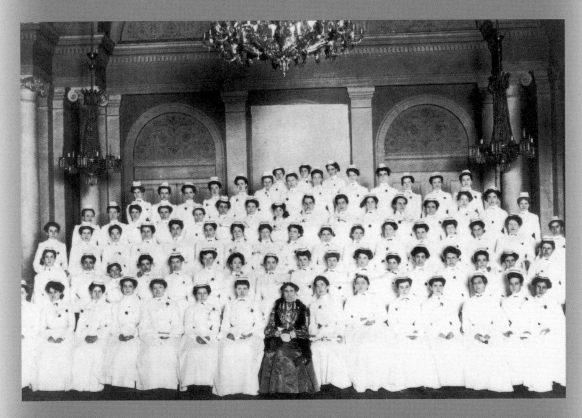

Even as she grew older, Clara Barton refused to give up her work as leader of the American Red Cross. Finally, in 1904 at the age of eighty-two, she resigned. She is pictured here with dozens of Red Cross nurses, probably around the time of her resignation.

In May 1904, at age eighty-two, Clara felt compelled to resign her office. She had served long and well. She moved to Glen Echo, Maryland, just outside Washington, D.C. There she spent her time writing and working on plans for an organization that would offer disaster relief in times of peace as well as in times of war.

When Clara Barton died at the age of ninety-one, she was buried in Oxford, Massachusetts. Americans hailed her as one of the country's greatest heroes. When she had seen a need, she had put all her strength into supplying that need. Clara did not live for herself alone. She devoted her life to helping others. Her legacy to the world, the American Red Cross, is a priceless gift destined to benefit future generations.

The Red Cross Today

Clara Barton reached her goals for the American Red Cross. Today a fifty-member board of governors directs the organization with national headquarters located in Washington, D.C. The organization's services are divided into several programs. These include a disaster services program, a nursing and health services program, and a safety services program. The Red Cross's blood services program is the largest blood donor service in the world.

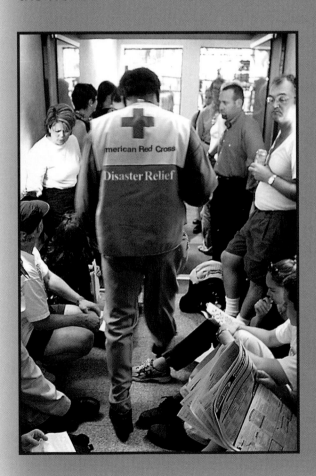

Today the Red Cross is known primarily as a disaster-relief organization. After the terrorist attacks of September 11, 2001, people lined up to donate blood at Red Cross blood banks across the United States. This picture was taken at a blood bank in Washington, D.C.

Important Dates

1821   December 25. Clarissa Harlowe Barton is born in North Oxford, Massachusetts.

1824   Can read at age three and starts school.

1838   Begins teaching career.

1852   Founds a successful free public school in Bordentown, New Jersey.

1854   Resigns from teaching when a man is put in charge of "her" school and she is expected to serve under him. Moves to Washington, D.C., and works at the U.S. Patent Office.

1861   Civil War begins. Clara volunteers to collect supplies for soldiers coming to the nation's capital.

1862   Travels to the battlefront to help wounded soldiers.

1864   Becomes an advocate for women's suffrage.

1865   Civil war ends and Clara sets up Bureau of Records to help reunite soldiers with their families. Travels to Andersonville, Georgia, prison to help mark graves.

1867	Begins a lecture circuit.
1870	Travels to Geneva, Switzerland, and hears about the International Red Cross. Franco-Prussian War breaks out in Europe, and Clara assists Red Cross workers.
1873	For her help in distributing supplies to wounded soldiers in France and Germany, Clara receives high honors including the Iron Cross of Merit from the emperor of Germany.
1881	Founds the American Red Cross and becomes its first president.
1881–1900	Travels to scenes of war-related disasters to help the victims.
1904	Resigns as president of the American Red Cross.
1912	April 12. Clara Barton dies.

For More Information

Books

King, David C. *First Facts About American Heroes.* Woodbridge, Connecticut: Blackbirch Press, Inc., 1996.

Nolan, Jeannette Covert. *The Story of Clara Barton of the Red Cross.* New York: Julian Messner, 1941.

Pryor, Elizabeth Brown. *Clara Barton: Professional Angel.* Philadelphia: University of Pennsylvania Press, 1987.

Web Sites

www.incwell.com/Biographies/Barton.html
www.civilwarhome.com/bartonbio.html
www.dansville.lib.ny.us/clara.html

Places to Visit

Clara Barton National
Historic Site
5801 Oxford Road
Glen Echo, MD
(301) 492-6245
www.nps.gov/clba

Clara Barton House
Dansville, NY
(716) 335-3500

Bibliography

King, David C. *First Facts About American Heroes.* Woodbridge, Connecticut: Blackbirch Press, 1996.

Mann, Peggy. *Clara Barton: Battlefield Nurse.* New York: Coward-McCann, Inc., 1969.

Nolan, Jeannette Covert. *The Story of Clara Barton of the Red Cross.* New York: Julian Messner, 1941.

Pryor, Elizabeth Brown. *Clara Barton: Professional Angel.* Philadelphia: University of Pennsylvania Press, 1987.

Quackenbush, Robert. *Clara Barton and Her Victory Over Fear.* New York: Simon & Schuster, 1995.

The Standard Reference Work. Volume 1. Progressive Educational Society. Chicago: Welles Brothers Publishing Company, 1913.

Whitelaw, Nancy. *Clara Barton: Civil War Nurse.* Springfield, New Jersey: Enslow Publishers, Inc., 1997.

Index